IN REAL LIFE

Poems

MAEGEN MCAULIFFE O'LEARY

THE FINISHED PROJECT

ISBN 979-8-9918767-5-9

THE FINISHED PROJECT

POETRY FOR REAL LIFE, IN REAL LIFE.

For Jack, as promised.

CONTENTS

IN REAL LIFE

Poet, In Real Life (27 July 2025)

IN REAL LIFE

I want to make something
markedly profitable. Nothing comes
from nothing and you can't sell nothing
except we do
all the time.

But this particular nothing
is non-fungible. A token
of appreciation for existing. I'm poor
like everyone I know
in real life. I wish it were different.

Genius comes to those through fate
but success does not
ride shotgun. You get the picture
I'm trying to paint. We're fucked.

I'm fucked. It's a big game
of fuck fucks and I
want to eat eggs and write
nothing the whole day long.

MERITOCRACY

I suppose no one is really ready
for it. Not any of it.

Does fortune favor the bold?
Or does fortune favor
the emboldened, their heads crowned
generationally with the angst of the masses?

I suppose they weren't ready
for it either.

What I am asking is
was I always doomed to fail
and didn't know it? The odds are

sure against me. Sure against those masses
I mentioned, who keep living
and dying, despite repeated attempts to stop
that nonsense. Life's a game of

existential kickball and I
suck at sports. Last picked
for every team. Worst luck
at lucky breaks.

It's a poor hen who won't scratch
for herself. Given everything

needed to survive
inside the game, I'd trade my life
to remember it now. To remember it now

I'd kill anything.

WHAT IF YOU'RE THE VILLAIN?

They say if you meet assholes

all day, you're the asshole—
you're the common
denominator in this simulation.
Top or bottom?

Denominator, I mean. I could never
remember my numerators
from my political agitators.
Strange times, these

cinematically filmed end
titles of an empire.
What's a Roman Empire
but a group of hairy white men thinking

time would stand still
if they ate enough cheese and shat marble
across naked earth? Here
for a good time, not a long time.

That tile mosaic looks lovely
beneath Golden Arches™.
Don't blame me,
I'm just the asshole recording it all

for posterity on my iPhone.

DEMI GOD

Memory wears us
as its skin. The doorway to heaven
sits in the eye. Once, I let a lame bird
die. Once, I asked a man to

prove he loved me. He could
not. I do not know why
we scrap and slash and dream.
My daughter dreamt she was horse

and all around her boys
knocked hammers on the water tower.
The town wait, flooded.
She reared and spat and watched them

all be swallowed by unsucked grief.
Grief snakes around us. Cuts from us
the knowledge that pain is finite.
Every choice made is a ripple

through reality. Half god,
we are. I've seen the wings.
All fluff and no future. Butterflies
trapped in meat.

HONORABLE MENTION

Every time the answer is no, ask
why not?

When you are mentioned, call it honorable
and allow the echo to bounce
between the walls of your pain—
back to those who give breath

for life inflating, out
to those who hold space
for life expanding, forward
to those who wait
for life advancing, and above

all, remember, we know nothing
we did not learn
from someone else.

We must speak our pain, so
another may hear us, calling:
You are not alone.

Together, we get free.

UNFAVORABLE CONDITIONS

Move from center, pause
before blow. A reckoning
is promised. A great gust
billows the sails. The wind

wants for nothing, except
to be caught, held
loosely, cheek cupped
and tendril stroked.

She howls
on arrival, body already
unfathomable
distance from sound.

UPRIGHT AND BREATHING

"Don't forget
the main point
is the main point,"
she said to me,

flicking to the next screen.
Don't forget
the soft underbelly
of prostrate arms,

the delicate arch
of hardwood heels.
Don't forget
all this—

hand swept
skyward, drunk bee
circling—
decays into stardust,

and elsewhere
is right here.
A warrior's heart,
a healer's hand.

One foot in shadow,
one in light.
Both upright
and breathing beneath me.

HOW TO START A REVOLUTION

Rest
so you can move.

Dream
so you can eat.

Breathe
so you can reach.

Stretch
so you can flex.

Rise
so you can follow

nothing
but your own true nature.

THE MUSHROOM TALKS BACK

Shut the fuck up.
Why are you
so loud all the time?
Stop searching

for what's buried
beneath you.
You wouldn't understand it
if you ate

every spongy body
in this joint.
You'll never kill us
in any way that matters.

BIRD SHIT

We don't exist
but in connection

to another. Isn't that
the saddest thing?

None of us are bad
or impossibly broken.

Given the chance,
we were all born

to fly, but we stay
crouched, arguing

over the taste
of clouds, dreaming

of open sky, clipping
each other's wings.

DON'T DIE WITH THESE THINGS

Still inside you:

your childhood phone number,
your reverence for birds,
your greatest achievement,
your anger at god,
your abandoned belief,
your faith in the trees,
your swiftest decision,
your obsession with dirt,
your once great and lovely
fear of the sky,
your deepest and darkest
shame on yourself,
your unfolded wings,
your uncorked tongue,
your terrible longing,
your most desperate whisper,
your kindest regret,
your weaponized rage,
your sharpest apology,
and your softest,
your truest,
your most helpless
yes.

THOUGHT PROCESS (CONVINCE ME OTHERWISE)

no no no no no no no no no no no no no no no
no no no no no no no no no no no no no no
no no no no no no no no no no no no no
maybe maybe maybe maybe maybe
maybe maybe maybe maybe
maybe maybe maybe
yes yes yes yes yes
yes yes yes yes
yes yes yes
I guess
so.

ANYTHING CAN BE POETRY

with a good title
and the right line break
s.

MEME

You think you are the world-
's savior, but really you are

just a confused corpse.

QUANTUM ENTANGLEMENT

Don't give up yet, dear one.
A tomb is opening

wide for you. A crack is forming
in the crust. Your light is coming,

catch the ride. The thrush won't kill
a thing, no matter how loud it blathers,

but the hummingbird flies
backward, forward, free

from space-time
and all manner of gravitational nonsense.

LÁ AN DREOILÍN

Don't look over your shoulder
for darkness following. Fly straight

into rain. Sunlit eyes beaconed
on mountain ash. Berry-breasted,

the druid's bird wins by climbing
and knowing when to break its fall.

Patience,
predator of the weak and sick,

patience.
The time for healing is at hand.

AN BRADÁN FEASA

Some days I have nothing but the promise
words will hurtle out of darkness.
Projectile dreams spawn upstream
as I weave my net
impatiently, determined
not to miss the catch.

GEALTACHT (AN INCANTATION)

Native plant,
local soil,
the only vessel
worth the toil.

Heather, feather,
stick and seed,
the proper cure
for unmet need.

THE EMIGRANT'S DAUGHTER

I want home so keenly,
this can't be my ache.
I don't have enough years for this
wanting of a thousand voices.

How many knees ached
in prayer spent frivolously? How many sighs
escaped parched lips? How many tongues
cut silent? The only coin too dear in value.

Imploring the impossible—to kiss the soil
that birthed your flesh, to go beneath the clay
with your mother's children, to return,
to root, to remain. To say

Brother, it took much
distance. Killed all save one, so
embrace me. Here I am, come
home at last.

THRESHOLD (IN THE DOORFRAME IS YOURSELF)

Sometimes you know things
before you should,
before you have a grip
on the collar of change.

Sometimes the backlit silhouette
in the doorframe is yourself,
practicing your exit
before latching closed the past.

HIT RECORD

In the quiet comes
God and all her armies,
led by the souls of lost
children, playing
their trumpets and banjos.
The music of death is a banger
tune. Angels weep
at the sound of the end. God laughs, hits
skip track and repents.

CAMERA OBSCURA

Real stars—holy
shit! We are both
still here.

SEARCH FOR INTELLIGENT LIFE

I learn to be comfortable with discomfort.
Thrust through the cracks of my body, I rise
high, and higher still. A rearranged atom

split lengthwise, all the secrets of the universe
gushing from my mouth to dry ears. A prayer
to the cosmos. A plea to infinity.

RELIC

At some point we become fiction.
A jumble of discarded objects
in the family attic. A half-smiled story,

stained tablecloth and crystal clock.
All mistakes and victories reduced
to a single photograph, occasionally

puzzled over, then slammed
back in the drawer
in time for Christmas dinner.

ON FACING DEATH

I hope you get
what your spirit came for.

I hope you are free.

ON TRUE LOVE

To watch the body
fail, but the spirit refuse.

To hold both in your hand
as they separate.

BUZZ KILL

Nature is never quiet, never
still. Only humans seek silence

in search of divine judgement,
but life is always humming.

It's death that makes no sound.

IRISH EXIT

All your pleading is for naught.
You never had any power
that did not come from her.

When she says it is time to leave
the party, we depart
without ceremony.

AFTER LIFE

How thin
the thread.

How wide
the threshold.

TAKE A NUMBER

Resist the lure to line up
for death. She does not take

the first in queue. Wait all night
for the door to loose, instead

earth opens,
swallows from below.

MOOD CONGRUENT MEMORY

There are no apologies
after death—there may be love,
there may be silence, but
regret is for the living.

So I disremember you.
It's not intentional, but my heart
prefers the softer you. My heart
prefers you as a child.

ACT [SUPER] NATURAL

I was born after the portal closed.
Meaning, I snuck through
when they were not watching
for escaping ghosts.

I rolled from grave to cave
in mountains left unguarded.
An uneasy apparition, haunting
skeptics in their nightshirts.

Such a godly thing, full of secrets
and confused silences.
I searched the earth for passage back,
tucked wings under my clavicle

but found only cobwebs,
dust prints on the family bible.
I whispered to worms, "Take me home!"
but they only writhed

under the root cellar, fixed
eyeless gaze upon me, then turned
back to the business at hand—
devouring death, digesting the entrails.

SOLSTICE, WINTER

You do not need a ticket
to the show. Light falls
on earth without you
there to swallow it.

Light falls.
Earth swallows.
Without you.
There.

Ticket, please.

A POEM FOR NEW YEAR'S DAY

The ball drops
on us while we sleep. Wolves feed
on garbage in the stream. Each swallow eats
the distance between reality
and death. No one asks if we deserve
to live. No one weeps
when wolves cease
howling at the wind. Us, we keep on
dreaming. Wolves wait
silent, hungry for our end.

SOUND BARRIER

A tree falls in the forest. I am
its obituary. No one reads anymore.

FORECAST

The shower of riches is about
to begin. Get wet,

then whetted. There is only
a small chance of rain.

RICH

Think I might
pierce my nose
with gold

sunlight

since I smell
rich and right
after rain.

ORIGAMI (WAKING FROM A DREAM ON FRIDAY)

XXX in one theater, patience in the other.
Whorl of blood on the penny, excrement

in the bowels. Bricked path to nowhere.
Singing hallelujah on Charon's bow.

Folding under paper envelopes—
a crane, a bullet, both flying at the greatest velocity

known to man. All blinking against the light.
It's an adjustment rising from the dark

to stand atop the clouds. No one lives forever.
We all want to die

right now. I let the words pass through me,
hoping my tongue will keep me proud.

LAMB

To cross the divide
between separateness and oneness, caress

the magnetic hum in your palm. Keep
unexpectedly still.

Childhood is humanity
not yet pitted against itself.

Magic is science
not yet explained.

God is love
not yet disappointed.

Body is compost
not yet earthwise.

Breath is fire
not yet kindled.

All of this is miracle
not yet witnessed.

APEX PREDATOR

The human smell of a place
is most animal
upon coming and going. Outside,

this is not us. Inside,
this is not either.
Somewhere, we left our savage musk

for the next beast to devour.
Somewhere, our home is
still wild.

FOSSIL FUEL

The world can really suck
the magic dry,
but the dinosaurs left
no stories
telling of the way
the world burned
full through the gut
of each creature,
so I may as well say
what I have to
because I am here.

POLARITY

I came out burning.
It was always going to be me.
Your death is a gift

dropped soundly in my lap.
Neatly bowed
and points just so.

I have a lot to say
about you,
about me,

about the way time stretches out
beyond the horizon, loops, drops,
circles back, spirals upward until

past, present, and future click together
like corresponding magnets
snapped into alignment with the stars.

BEAT BOX

You see that, there—
That pulsing?

That's it.
That's you.
That is your life.

And it will not keep
such time forever.

So hope, hope!

The next beat will not be
the final drum.

LET IT BE REMEMBERED

that I swore constantly. That I'd die
before admitting defeat. That I'd laugh
before admitting guilt. That never once did I
miss an opportunity
to turn each moment into something
as silly as a poem.

IN GOOD COMPANY

Maybe that is all
death is—me,
talking to myself
for eternity.

ACKNOWLEDGEMENTS

Early versions of many of these poems appeared on TheFinishedProject.org and on social media accounts belonging to the author and The Finished Project.

"Act [Super] Natural" was initially published in Taboo Tribune's *Dead of Fall – Issue 02* (2023).

ABOUT THE AUTHOR

Maegen McAuliffe O'Leary is a poet and artist from the Pacific Northwest. Her work focuses on the contemporary human experience as it intersects feminism, matrimony, motherhood, magic, creative expression, and the human body and its place in nature. She is the author of *Bodies to Bury the Hunger* (2022); *Full Belly: Poems* (2024); *Richest Bastard in the Poorhouse: Poems for the Proletariat* (2025); *Stuffed: Love Poems for Assholes* (2025); and *In Real Life* (2026).

McAuliffe O'Leary is the founder of The Finished Project, a creative communications company inspired by the sacred feminine forces of creativity, courage, compassion, and communication. The Finished Project supports living artists and women-owned, small business through an online retail platform that promotes poetry for real life, in real life. Visit TheFinishedProject.org to learn more.

POETRY FOR REAL LIFE, IN REAL LIFE.

www.ingramcontent.com/pod-product-compliance
Lightning Source LLC
La Vergne TN
LVHW090537110826
845146LV00003B/1153